THE BOOK EATERS

The
BOOK EATERS

Carolina
Hotchandani

perugia
PRESS

FLORENCE, MASSACHUSETTS
2023

Copyright © 2023 by Carolina Hotchandani

Perugia Press extends deeply felt thanks to the many individuals whose generosity made the publication of *The Book Eaters* possible. Perugia Press is a tax-exempt, nonprofit 501(c)(3) corporation publishing first and second books of poetry by women. To make a tax-deductible donation, please contact us directly or visit our website.

Book design by Jeff Potter and Rebecca Olander

Author photograph by Mark Munger

Cover, title page, and part title page art by Elizabeth Munger: Mixed media: acrylic paint, pen and ink, sekishu paper, found book pages (source: *Swann's Way, Remembrance of Things Past*, Volume One, Marcel Proust, translated from the French By C. K. Scott Moncrieff, New York: Henry Holt and Company, 1922).

Library of Congress Cataloging-in-Publication Data

Names: Hotchandani, Carolina, 1979- author.
Title: The book eaters / Carolina Hotchandani.
Other titles: Book eaters (Compilation)
Description: Florence, MA : Perugia Press, 2023. | Summary: "In Carolina Hotchandani's debut The Book Eaters, the poet's desire for agency over her life's narrative is counterbalanced by her awareness that poetry is written precisely when life wrests control from us. This book, conceived in loss, examines shifts in identity due to Partition, immigration, illness, and birth. As roles evolve and dissolve, the poet witnesses the decay of language, artifacts, and history, yet these erasures are also generative: they beget poetic creation. The Book Eaters is a study in belonging as well-to our bodies, our memories, our stories, ourselves, our families, our cultures. Hotchandani's poems interrogate what it means to be full or empty (of words, of the past, of another human being); they illuminate our inextricability from our creaturehood. Even as they explore unraveling- through the metaphor of insects that devour the very pages we produce-these poems are tightly woven into an exquisitely crafted, cohesive collection"-- Provided by publisher.
Identifiers: LCCN 2023031297 | ISBN 9780997807677 (paperback)
Subjects: LCGFT: Poetry.
Classification: LCC PS3608.O839 B66 2023 | DDC 811/.6--dc23/eng/20230710
LC record available at https://lccn.loc.gov/2023031297

Perugia Press
PO Box 60364
Florence, MA 01062
editor@perugiapress.org
perugiapress.org

For my dear parents—one in this world, one in my memories.

Vera Ellen de Araujo Hotchandani
&
Manohar Hotchandani (1939-2022)

CONTENTS

III *A Family of Trees*

I

MEMORY, HALVED

PORTRAIT OF APHASIA ON A PLUM TREE

Was it not then—as you reached for a word like a ball you'd kicked high
into the plum tree's grasp, and failing to seize it, said, *Forget it*,
so the word stayed there
suspended with the overripe plums warming in the sun beside the nest of a bird
neither of us could name (though the problem of forgetting
was not mine)—

Was it not then that silence filled the space where the word
might have bounced like this, like here, like so
and so I left my body like a ball in motion
as the absence of your thought condensed
into a pit (as of a plum) I swallowed
till it burrowed in my chest like a solid thing
a word could almost name.

LANGUAGE, A MEAL I THOUGHT WE SHARED

In the beginning, the gesture occurs
without a thought:

I reach for the word you
can't grasp and pass it to you
like a bowl filled with rice.

You spoon the rice onto your plate
and pass back the empty bowl.

Here, the rounded space
the bowl surrounds
is not an image of loss.

PARTITION

In your version of the story, people butter their fingers
with notions of God, splitting India into a smaller India,
a new Pakistan. The way a single *roti's* dough
is pulled apart, the new spheres, rolled in the palms,
then flattened. *The idea of God—the destroyer of human bonds,*
you will say—*the reason for new borders, new*
pain to sprout on either side of a dividing line. You'll go on.
I'll picture the edges of your words blurring to a hum
as I think of how to wrest your rant from you.
A rolling pin barrels over dough, widens the soft disk,
makes it fine. You are fragile. Like a story that stretches
belief. Like a nation. Like a thin disk of dough that sticks
to a surface, tearing when it's peeled back. I don't know
how to part the story from the person and keep the person.

THE STORIES THAT TOLD YOU

As memory falters, stories tell and retell themselves
through my father's mouth. They're in charge.
Like a skilled ventriloquist with a hand
in his head. I remember the tales
I begged him, as a child, to tell again, *please*—
the ones whose animal characters he'd make squeak
to make me laugh. I'd ask for the one
with the lion who wrestles with the hunter's net,
tangling himself further in his adversary of mesh.
Till a mouse happens by, who, with small, sharp teeth,
frees the beast from the story's trap.
I remember my father whetting his voice to a needle's point
to pass through the mouse and speak for him:
Never underestimate those you see as weak.
As stories now insert themselves between my father
and his voice, I wish I could make myself fine,
like the mouse's cuspate teeth—to sever
the insides of stories, release my father.

AUTHOR UNKNOWN

There's a story that rolls daily
over the streets of my father's mind—
its asphalt enameled with rain.

A bus treads through a puddle
that fights gravity as the bus halts
and hisses, wets my father's shirt.

Doors part. He steps in, unaware
the bus carries the woman
he'll marry. My mother.

A light turns green. The story accelerates—
jostling the strangers inside
till the bus jolts to a stop:

a passenger's flung
onto my father's lap. My mother
smiles; a conversation

starts: neither of them is meant
to be in Rio that day. Today,
my father quotes Newton

as he narrates this tale:
inertia made that passenger fall,
as motion always wants to stay

in motion. But who grayed the skies—
who made the rain percuss
Rio's rooftops like an amateur drummer

so no one could go on foot
that day? I want to know
who authored the story

driven by the bus
that set us in motion—
my family, on its course.

THE BOXES

We move. We move every few years. What's made of glass
        we wrap in newspaper, boxing
memories that, for others, live in hometowns. Their memories
        are perennials, sprouting thoughts
of years before, when holes were dug, when kids couldn't decide
        between irises and alliums,
then the irises won, petaling memories of arguments, reconciliations.
        Purpling that summer. We move
in trucks, in boxes, our contents: four continents and who knows how
        many cities, rooms, drawers.
How many corners of us are emptied in the new town, free
        of the objects left
at the last town's Goodwill. We miss the goodwill of old friends.
        Memories stretch
from the last place, the way I reached for an apple at the old
        grocery store—the whole
pyramid of them toppling over, bruised, rolling. Memories of things
        falling do not exist in neat
arrangements on display tables. They do not gleam on the waxed skins
        of Red Delicious apples,
assembled in the same spot in the same store we'd visit for years.
        We don't have the years.
We store the store, our memories rolling to the next town, where some
        sense of not belonging lives under
my hot cheeks as I overhear a girl tell another girl, *The eyebrows
        of the new girl are like the tail
of a squirrel.* I hear the giggles. I feel the apples, bruised, rolling
        through my body, which is
no grocery store. The floor of me does not shine. I am not lit
        with bright lights. I am the boxes
we take to the next place, which tear and are taped. When my father
        starts to forget, I understand.
The places never held us. We hold the places. We move.

POSSIBLE CONSOLATION OF A BRAIN SCAN'S TOPOGRAPHY

On the scan: a flattened ridge, a valley grown wide—
a smoothness that explains

the gaps.

My father and I took a road trip once—
California through the Rockies
to the Great Plains.

The outer layer of his brain
is like Nebraska, where I
live now.

I could find comfort in this:
flat land surrounds me,
blanketed with corn.

He doesn't remember the trip,
but he's here with me
anyhow.

SELF-PORTRAIT AS THE CORNFIELDS

As the past recedes from memory, I retrace my steps. I am a citizen of a former British colony that rebelled from England with a great tea party, declaring itself its motherland. America. Was it orphaned? Did it kill its own mother? Poor England. *Where are you from?* the other Americans ask me. *My mother is Brazilian; my father is Indian. I was born in Brazil, but I've been here a long while. Here where? Here here.* Here New York, Texas, North Carolina, Tennessee, Rhode Island, a year abroad in England, then California, Iowa, Texas again, then a year in South Korea, then Chicago, then another "South," but this time South Dakota, which isn't in this country's South at all. Now Nebraska. *Here here*, where the cornfields stretch from the highway to the horizon. *Here here*, where corn is fed to cattle who don't graze. *Hear, hear!* as they shout in the House of Commons, to affirm the speaker's thoughts. *Hear, hear!* to the English that seems foreign. *Hear, hear!* to the rustle of corn that doesn't belong here. *Hear, hear!* to the language I use to build this block of words, which you may not hear at all, if you are quiet, if you follow the lines with your eyes, unspeaking, like mine, as they trace the rows of corn in the fields. Fed to the cows that Indians know as holy. Fed to the cows the Americans know as beef. I will become your cornfields, striped, farmed, not native at all, but everywhere, everywhere.

SONETTO

Somehow history finds its ways to pass through us.
I was a toddler, enthralled as you dunked the metal globe
into your steaming cup—as the water surrounding the sphere
turned gold, like that crescent of sky that touches the sun
as it rises. Later, I'll learn of high tea, Empire, the colonies.
You'll recall the day India's independence was declared:
you ate *ladoo, jalebi*. A child full of glee. Till you left home,
made another home, a new language testing itself on your tongue.
Poverty callused your feet, bore holes through your shoes.
You crossed an ocean, built a life. As memory caved, the past
became your shelter. I, too, turn back to the past—preserved
in that stained cup where you poured the milk, clouding the amber
as you sang "Tea for Two" and bounced me on your knee. Always
that same little song as I wobbled—a child on one of history's limbs.

ONCE YOU TURN EIGHTY-TWO

I find myself mining you for the history
you lived through—
mining you the way they
suck from the earth to make theirs
the coal, the gold—the way they steal, too,
the wind from air—

I extract from the subcutaneous
reservoir of history your life obscures
(like grass and soil over oil)
the events I know as bullet points
on textbook timelines—

and why, if I find the bullet points dry and dead,
would I condense you into dots on a line—

if not for that they call this *knowledge*,
say *I have it* (and plus, you are fading),
and *it's mine.*

THE CULPRIT

As you finish your morning cup of tea,
an identity thief rings.

You answer.

Sleep wraps loosely around your mind
like the flannel robe you're still wearing.

It's almost noon.

The television is on
but muted.

On the screen, Lieutenant Columbo's mouth moves
as he pesters his prime suspect.
Soon, he'll reveal how the murderer
murdered the murdered.

You answer the phone.
The voice on the other end
dubs over the episode's denouement:
Tell me the story behind your name.
So you do.
Can you spell it for me?
So you enunciate:
M as in "money"- A - N as in "Nancy"- O - H...
till all the letters of your name go down
into the small holes of the phone.

You were born in India before Partition?
Those were hard times.

When the voice solicits your Social Security number,
you want to know why,
but the logic you're offered makes sense:
there's money to be claimed
by survivors of arduous times.

Columbo lights his cigar.
The murderer's exposed, and the credits are rolling.

The end is not surprising; we've known it from the start.

We won't learn who trafficked in your memories,
committing this crime.
You aren't the best witness,
forgetful these days.
You watch and rewatch your favorite TV sleuth
intuit the culprit, apprehend the truth.

PORTRAIT OF APHASIA ON A BURNISHED MOON

Was it not then, as you thudded over memory's potholes
embarrassed for swerving too late, I searched for ways
that your forgetting echoed mine. A word effaced itself
in a conversation, I told you, and then I caught a glimpse
of my idea's underside, like a deer the darkness hid
till the moon appeared and all I saw was movement.
A flash of being. It was the word "eclipse," of all words,
that escaped me like that furtive deer—its hind legs
springing over brush. I was left with the white tail
of a thought in a sentence: *The moon moved
into the Earth's shadow*, which surrounded my idea
while obscuring it, the way the conifer forest
embraces the deer while sheltering it from human eyes.
Pine needles must have brushed my fragile thought as it left me
and I flushed, like that strange and rare and reddish moon.

WORMHOLES

Sometimes I believed the future lived
under the surface
of the present,

and if I tried, I could
unveil it. The way my mother
peeled back the artichoke's scales,

paring away a light fuzz
to reach the heart.
Lately, I'm afraid of the cores

I find strewn across the counter.
My father's eating peaches,
cherries, plums.

So many bananas.
He even tries to eat the peels.
I remember how he'd prick

his finger each day—
a globule of blood rising
from beneath this moment

to its outer tip. He'd stamp
his blood onto a strip to learn
if he was fine.

Now he takes in the sweetness
he'd always feared.
As a child

I shuddered at that lance,
that scarlet sphere.
I worry: his worry's gone.

Tira as minhocas da cabeça,
my mother says.
Pull those worms out of your head.

Imagined futures:
I need you to stay under
the grass, wriggling deep in the Earth.

Close to its unknown core.

NESTING

When the birds' names doubled with words that summoned
ideas from their hiding places (the *flicker*, the *chat*, the *swift*, the *lark*),
I watched them more closely, confident that somewhere
a thought would escape the bird, alighting upon a pun,
and I'd find meaning in a world that glided
above me, hardly dipping into my mind.
When I saw a swallow's nest balanced on a truss
like an idea teetering upon a word,
I waited for the mother-swallow to return
with her twigs, her morsel of mud, her blade of glass.
What idea would nestle there?
Later, as the babies pecked themselves out of shells,
I saw their open-beaked pleas, wondered
at their desperate mouths and how they swallowed.
I believed in no gods, and when words with different meanings
echoed themselves, I felt I lived inside a poem someone else had made,
and I rhymed with every bird on my line.

SPIRES

A year floats up from a parent's mind
like a hot-air balloon the sky
let slip away.

A spot of crimson in a blue expanse.

My twenty-first year buoys itself in the distance:

I lived in England then—
a young woman, learning desire,
learning how men saw
and didn't see me.

The father I had then
had a strikingly good memory.

Today, my parents and I sit around a circular table,
sipping tea at a wedding reception.
A centerpiece of lilies trumpets its yellow scent into our air.

My father brings up the year I spent abroad—
in France, he says.
In the company of others,
I don't correct him.

What have I lost
as my father misplaces a year of my life—
a year that was anyway
long passed,
gone—

shrouded in my mind like Gothic domes in the English clouds
till my father's misremembrance
pricks the sky of my mind
like the spires of Oxford's cathedrals.

They seem to puncture
whatever those low English clouds
were always hiding.

A LITTLE WATER

The rain comes down and prompts the world's thrumming.

Outside, leaves escape their trees,
pasting themselves on windshields.

Dislocated pieces of the world
skim the sidewalks, lawns.

A paper bag—hooked on the wind's hooks—
reels above the grass.

Memories float up against the downpour
like leaves from my father's reused tea bags.

My childhood browns the cup.

When you were in France for one year,
my father says, and I correct him.
I was in England, not in France.
Do you remember the tea I brought back for you?

And, *Oh yes,* he then recalls
or finds his faith in the story I tell.
I offer it to him:
my past—a gift of tea.
A souvenir from a place not here.

Muddy water trickles in through cracks in the basement floor,
forming tributaries that join at a point,
so a river flows through my home.

I think of the English Channel—
how some people swim across it
from France to England.

What difference does a little water make?

ETERNAL PISTACHIOS

I begin to write, aiming to capture flecks of the past
your mind discards.

I take note of a note you wrote yourself
and slipped into your pocket.

> 1. *Buy bananas.*
> 2. *Stop buying pistachios.*

Bags of husked pistachios are piling up in the pantry,
and you've just bought more. Your note, forgotten.
Tossed out like empty shells.

Those packages of shelled green nuts stuffed into our shelves
call up a photograph I saw in a *National Geographic* once.

Turtles studded a black rock in the middle of the ocean.

They absorbed sunlight like faceted gems—
dark green jade
upon onyx.

Stretching their necks upward,
they seemed to yearn
for the sun's gaze.

I place those turtles in this poem—
here—
reaching to be seen, remembered.

I KEEP SEARCHING FOR THE PERFECT METAPHOR

for memory loss. Some days, insects that ravage books
are all I write about. Spinning the metaphor's threads
around me, I undergo a metamorphosis—
closed off, for a while, from the metaphor's tenor,
which lingers above the page
like a delicate cocoon hanging from a twig—

I focus on the vehicle—
on the segmented exoskeletons of the insects,
on their legs, their roving antennae,
so rife with minute detail,
on how they consume entire archives of human knowledge,
some grazing the pages' edges, some boring straight through
like they want to shovel out the heart of a living thing—

then I remember the tenor—
and oh, how I wish I knew more about opera,
so I read about the great tenors and forget,
for some time, that I am writing about forgetting.

SILVERFISH, *LEPISMA SACCHARINA*

When I am present, they are hiding.
In their absence, I gather facts about the insects
from the books that don't harbor them.
I learn how the female silverfish lays a cluster
of soft, white eggs between pages,
imparting to the unhatched nymphs
shelter and nourishment in a single object:
the book will be their home,
the pages, their source of starch
and protection from the bright lights.
Every few days they will feed and molt,
feed and molt into the future,
shedding scales of silver powder
like those who can't bear the flashing
presence of the past.

I BECOME A HISTORIAN

as my father repeats his questions,
forgets my answers—
as the years of my life become the wrinkles
his brain irons out.

I look for fabrics that easily crease—
linens, fine silks,
any cloth a single gesture crumples.

Remember this gesture, I want to say.

Fold and pleat and furrow yourself
as though we've shared a history.

As though it's made a mark.

CASEMAKING CLOTHES MOTH, *TINEA PELLIONELLA*

As they feed, the larvae of casemaking clothes moths spin silken tubes that wrap around their bright white bodies. Beadlike, amber heads poke out of these tunnels as they graze on fabric, but if something disturbs them—a cold breeze rippling through the room, a bright light—they abscond wholly into their woven encasements, which conceal them, as they are the color of the fabric consumed. When the larvae nestle inside a book, it is the binding (made sometimes of a woolen thread) or the cover (made of animal hide) that attracts them, containing the keratin they seek. The larvae open their jaws to consume strands of wool, thinning the yarn gradually, till the book's pages are no longer joined—till the human utterances fall, out of order, onto the floor. There our histories lie, a pile of leaves descended from many trees, with no connection between them. After pupation, the larvae transform into moths: they cease to have mouths and eat nothing. Silken scrolls and unbound pages mark their presence, making the case that creatures with mouths once lived there.

HOW CAN IT BE—

my father reaching for a peach
when he ate two in the last hour.
Satiation depends on the memory
of eating, I learn. My mother
scolds him: two dozen
mandarins, bought yesterday,
are gone. What my father needs
is to be fed the past. I try.
Here is my recollection of your meal:
here, my immaterial crumbs
of your morning bread. Pierce,
with a fork's tines, this slice of melon
I make of words and offer
to a mind that keeps rumbling.
Time's become a food
your body can't digest.

MEMORY, HALVED

I remember creating an edible model
of a cell when I was twelve.

My parents helped. We gathered
jelly beans, dry noodles,

poppy seeds. In a clear,
round casserole dish, peach Jell-O

congealed, turned
to cytoplasm. Circus peanuts

from last year's Halloween
metamorphosed into mitochondria—

"the powerhouse of the cell,"
my textbook said, as they extract

energy from food, deriving,
from one substance, another.

We are always making doubles
of what exists—replicas

of real things, memories that try
to copy experience even as they tweak

the color of a dress, the weather
the day of a funeral, and whether

we were even there at all. I remember
fashioning the nucleus from a hard-

boiled egg I cut in two. I know,
even as my father forgets whole

years of my life, that I am more
than partly loved. But I recall my shock

when he reached for the half
of the nucleus I didn't use

and took a bite—

II

THE MAKING OF MIRRORS

SO THE HUMANS REPRODUCED

For the world required another mirror—
proffered by the eyes of the child.
For the ocean was insufficient.
For the water on windy days withheld reflections,
giving back the crests of waves—
their foam and spray—
and nothing more.
For the mirrors, chiseled and polished by hands,
were flat, so the humans whirled before the glass
in search of the third dimension.
For children's eyes were curved
like the Earth the sun lit daily.
For children cried as light pierced their eyes,
and what the humans heard was need.
It was not theirs. It was theirs.
It was the truest reflection they could almost see.

CHIAROSCURO

Against the sonogram's black background, bones
glow like fragments of distant nebulae:
starlike hands, moonlike head, cratered where eyes
will later be set. I hold my camera
above the image; I want a photo
to send to my mom. There is no angle
that lets me capture this cluster of bones
from which the eye divines a human form.
The glossy finish reflects the lamp's light—
a white nimbus: the baby's twin, conceived
of light, without consent. What worlds entered
me, undiscerned? What annunciation
follows? I feel a stirring of stars. I
wait for hidden lives to be delivered.

A VASE ON A SHELF

I fall into a purple sleep, and your mumbles, which are likely words,
become the meaning of *purple*
as a word is cast aside—
a vase you forgot on a shelf and filled with nothing.

Place it here,
beside the cast-off word—
right here

where a faraway viola plays notes that echo the violets in the field
as well as a grape in a different field (I think a Concord)
which falls, overripe, from the vine to the grass.

I will become a mother soon,
and the baby leaving my body will be the purple
that leaves the word, the stem, the vine.

BECAUSE I HEAR SHE HEARS ME FROM THE WOMB

I read my favorite passages aloud
hoping my love of them passes
through skin and blood

and the walls of the womb.
I gather the frayed edges of my being
and streamline myself

to enter the book,
to move with the current
of another's voice—

I, a raft on its freshet of sound,
headed somewhere important—
somewhere large and encompassing.

Momentum builds,
powered by I am not sure what.
A lack of stops—

a dilation of syntactic units—
and I'm a character in an eighteenth-century novel,
blushing and aflutter.

Words, evenly spaced
on the page, belie
clustering referents:

mushrooms springing up from moist earth,
monarchs flocking to the bark,
mottling an ashen trunk

as if by orange lichens.
Then I fly
out of the book—

glancing at how light grates itself
against the blinds, falling
in strips on strips of hardwood floor.

This strange body of mine
will divide itself in some
weeks' time, to birth

a body, to feed
that body, splitting itself
again as I read and inhabit

the lives inside a book.
You, who listen to my voice
sliding into the author's

as a knife does into its sheath—
you will tear through this
chamber of sound—

I will scream as never
I had, and you'll cry a cry
that will be no one's,

and your own.

SNOW ABOVE SNOW

The sky bears down and then divides.
A blizzard is born.
Snow above snow above snow—
the ground rises to meet the sky,
or the other way around.
We're in the car, heading to the hospital
atop clouds that billow out
when a rabbit darts into the white.
We swerve but don't miss.
Today my daughter meets the world
upside down.
Today a rabbit buries itself in a sky.

THE THING ON THE BED

I am lying on the hospital bed, and my left hand touches a plastic bag full of fluid that seems too hot to be in plastic. The bag is next to my leg. I ask the nurse what it is. *Where?* she asks. I put my hand on it to show her. She lifts up the sheet. *That's your leg*, she says. When she leaves the room, I ask my husband to make sure. He looks and confirms the thing is my leg. I press it directly with my left palm, then the back of that palm, then my fingertips. The leg does not feel my hand, which is unsurprising, but my hand, which has not lost its senses, insists the leg is not a leg. The hand creates a picture in my mind that is false, according to the witnesses, yet I believe its testimony: on the bed, there is a bag full of the fluids one requires for life—plasma, blood, etc. I imagine it will supply me with what labor has depleted. My charitable leg, a donor of sorts, standing with and for me, the way legs do. And it stands for *me*, like a good synecdoche for the good poet, summoning the whole with a single part. I am a thing full of the fluids of life. Later, milk will spring from hidden ducts; breasts will weep. Outside me, there will be crying, and inside, I will wonder if it is mine or another's.

WASH THAT MAN RIGHT OUT OF MY HAIR

> Now it happened that Metis was going to have a daughter, and she sat
> inside Zeus's head hammering out a helmet and weaving a splendid robe
> for the coming child. Soon Zeus began to suffer from pounding headaches
> and cried out in agony. All the gods came running to help him, and skilled
> Hephaestus grasped his tools and split open his father's skull. Out sprang
> Athena, wearing the robe and the helmet, her gray eyes flashing. Thunder
> roared and the gods stood in awe.
>
> — Ingri and Edgar Parin D'Aulaire, "Athena"

I've never met the doctor who happens to be on call when I go into
labor. A sweet-smelling aftershave precedes him into the delivery
room. *We're gonna get that baby right out of you*, he says, pulling a latex
glove over one hand and stretching the opening wide so it snaps back
with a loud smack against his wrist. I want those hands nowhere near
me. I imagine him coaching Little League, tapping his baseball cap
to send signals to tiny players in the outfield. He chews gum for the
entirety of my labor. After I push with all my might for three-and-a-
half hours and the baby has still not moved, he says with a half-wink,
Poor thing. You'll be so sore when this is all over.

The baby's been out of me for a while now,
but that man is still inside.

I go over what's happened again and again,
desperate to find the angle through which
he exits the scene and stays gone:

He sees himself from the outside: a hero who enters the scene *in
medias res*, scenting the room with sweet nectars. He will stop in,
introduce himself, and smile his neighborly smile before he sets off
on a journey through the hospital. Doors will open, doors to women
splayed on beds. Women writhe; women scream in pain. Some will be

monstrous—Scyllas and Charybdises among them. Their wounds will gape. Their wombs will pull against his virile strength, for they hold the center of the Earth within them; theirs, the blood of the wine-dark sea. He tells himself, *Do not waver; do not let their currents steer you. Skate above the dark waters. Wait to come through the door when they quake, when they halve. Stand back till they split in two. Then sew them up, and it's you, it's you who's made them new!*

Pull that man right out of my head.
Let me be Zeus on that hospital bed.

IN THE BEGINNING

As the baby pulled the cold air into her lungs,
I saw a nurse take her tiny foot,
press it into a pad of blue ink,

and write with her body

her body

as if my baby were, at once,
the pen and the word.

ACHILLES SEES LIFE LEAVING FROM HIS HEEL

The nurse asked me if I could raise my legs yet.

I watched my feet to see if they'd move when I tried.
The right one twitched a bit.

The little one
must have been taken somewhere before then
to get a shot or have blood drawn.

Later, I would see how
they draw blood from a baby. A needle stuck
in the heel, of all places.

All I know is
her cry was not in the room
as I tried to find
my will in my legs.

Sometimes I think
she took it away. My baby,
my will. As if she drew it out of my

bony heel.

PHANTOM

> Nearly every man who loses a limb carries about with him a constant or inconstant phantom of the missing member, a sensory ghost of that much of himself.
>
> —Silas Weir Mitchell, *The Injuries of Nerves and Their Consequences*

Tonight I awake in a fright, gripping my left arm with my right
as though my arm is a baby
falling out of my arm. I need to
break the fall.

Later my husband tells me I'd handed him
my arm while sleeping to ask if he'd hold her
while I went to the bathroom.

Descartes writes of how some "feel pain
in the parts they no longer possess."

I've not lost an arm,
yet a ghost has lodged itself
in my left one.

These nights, I drop
and catch and drop it again.

It does not cry
when it hits the floor.

A CORD TO BIND US

Was it not then, as I saw the future embodied

in the body of my child, I sought a story

to tether us together—my daughter, myself—

a story, too, to tie the mother-me

to the one I was before I birthed her.

The cord had been severed.

Then I heard a woman ask,

Is that white baby yours?

as if all I was was not

white, as if all my daughter was was white,

as if I were a brown

wet nurse feeding the baby

the only white drops of me—

SELF-PORTRAIT AS A WOMAN HALVED

What seems a long time ago, a line of pigment
drew itself down the middle of my torso—
linea nigra, splitting the globe of my belly
into hemispheres: I am East, and I am West,
child of parents from both sides of the world.
Brazil is my mother's motherland.
Land of the *pau-brasil*, the tree that gave
the country its name—its red sap
extracted by those who were enslaved. They
powdered the sap to make a dye, connoting
power in European fabrics. Power powder.
My father is Indian—land of cinnamon
and clove, land of spices the Portuguese
sailed East for, land of the tea the English
mass-produced so that Indians
now drink it with milk, as my father does,
as I've learned to do. The line that breaks me
in two is neater than I thought natural things
could be. Once the baby's born, the thin strip
slowly fades. But I'll look at my child—
her skin whiter than mine—
and feel divided. Afraid the world
will grant her an ease that keeps her
from knowing me. Glad, too,
for that same reason.

CURSIVE

My mother visits
as soon as the baby is born.
She makes me food to make me
make milk.

She sautées onions, tomatoes, collards.

They rise and hang in the air, slinking into other rooms

where my childhood sits at a table
practicing cursive *q*'s,
noticing no labor whose ghosts
scent the air I breathe.

I do not write often of my mother.

I become a mother.

Still, I make myself
the child curling ink into
words to keep
from disappearing.

RECURSIVE

My mother scrubs my tea-stained robe white

when she visits, white as one of my father's shirts

whose stains she blanches on a clothesline in the sun—

white as the wedding dresses I rejected in the bridal boutique

where I chose a dress of silk, dyed, as if by tea.

She rubs clean the terrycloth robe till it's a memory

of a spill, erased—a new beginning for a new mother

who feels otherwise far from the daughter she is—

the daughter I am—as I collect my baby's clothes,

stuff them in the washing machine, and when the whites

come out with stains abiding, I leave them that way,

for there are no beginnings. We carry on.

MOTION PICTURE

The sidewalk extends in front of us:
a strip of celluloid film.

It's my first stroll outdoors with the baby.
My father decides he'll join us
once I've enveloped her with swaddling blankets,
once he's checked their warmth and found them wanting,
once I've layered my coat around this dense cocoon.

We take two steps onto our first slab of concrete.
He halts my forward progress and points:
Look at that seam in the sidewalk
that's not doing its job—
its caulking thinned by winter salts.
Like this, we take steps forward till we reach an edge.
We pause. We stay inside our frame.

There we are, inside the motion picture before the motion is perfected—
arrested in the frame where the tree's roots spread farther
than anyone foresaw, pushing upward against the sidewalk
till it cracks the ground beneath our feet—

and my father curses the tree's arrogance
and our tax dollars' impotence
and the people who didn't know
what the tree would predictably do:
search, like all of us, for a bit of ground for support.

Then he locks arms with me and keeps the film reeling—
tells me to walk,
but watch my step.

BOOK OF VIOLETS

When I was a character in a book
someone was writing,
I gazed up at a storied sky

whose planets were globe-shaped
ideas that orbited a mind
I did not know.

Once, I saw a falling star
the author of the sky
erased the moment I pointed at it,

mesmerized for an instant
at a thing I thought
I might create a world around.

Some days I felt a dull ache,
perhaps a memory, perhaps
an imagined past outside the book,

when I had seen myself a maker
of characters such as the one I was.
Inside the book, I was a woman—

a wife, a mother, a daughter.
Outside the book I had been
only a woman.

What the difference was,
I tried to discover,
recalling some violets I had placed

in the middle of a thick novel once.
The past and future they lay between
had pressed them flat

so they commingled with the page:
words appeared through
papery petals, purple veins.

What was ink; what was the pigment of petals?
When I was only a woman, I was able
to distinguish between things.

My father had begun to forget
my youth, and I viewed
my story now through the tint of a mind

undoing itself, undoing me,
the way ribbons of light that seem
like shooting stars taper

till they're swallowed by the sky.
On days when a gloomy mood
was present in my world,

I gazed at my daughter and saw her
as the future incarnate,
bearing the form and weight

of being already written,
already mingled with my petaled self
that bled its blood across the page.

SENSE AND SENSIBILITY

In an hour, my seminar begins. Pumping the breast milk
that threatens to burst, I prepare. Shut the door.
Lower the shades. Turn on soft tunes
to preserve the good opinion of the professor next door,
who will not hear the *Eeee uhhh eeee uhhh* of the pump.
Top secret business here. I think of Austen
as I watch the bottle fill up with bluish-white fluid—
how the women in her books who dote on children
are always the insipid, the vacuous ones.
Anne and Lucy Steele, Lady Middleton—
women who spoil children with sugarplums, sweetmeats,
gifts of ribbon—women who praise every squeak a child lets out.

I'll ask the class why they're in the novels at all:
is it to highlight, through contrast,
the heroines' talents of reflection and expression,
or are the flat characters dispensable?

There's nothing left to express. I wrap the bottle in an ice pack.
If I don't get home within three hours, I'll have to get rid of it.

LAW OF CONSERVATION OF MASS AND ENERGY

As vapor looms over hot water not
yet turned to steam, I hover above this
body: *There she is—a woman nursing.*
I watch a small mouth rooting at the breast.

Milk, milk, everywhere. Not a thought to think.
As the baby drinks from my body my
milk, I edit my manuscript, clipping
lines, aborting whole poems, tearing out

pages from my notebook as if each spot
of ink erased is a drop of milk saved
for the baby. There is only this much
of me. Matter is not created, not

destroyed. I can balance this equation:
I feel the letdown. My thoughts turn to milk.

REAL ESTATE

In class, a student of mine quotes Heidegger:
Every man is born as many men
and dies as a single one.
He moves on, pontificates on poetry,
claiming the air around us—
an estate he'll soon inherit.
My mind can't register the new sounds
his mouth makes as I think of every woman
I know and whether Heidegger's aphorism
applies. I am a professor and new mother
who hears the boy say, *Heidegger said,*
and he becomes Heidegger as well as himself,
while I am one woman in the middle
of all the men making word sounds.

JESUS ENVY

Thought birthed Descartes in an empty room
where no one cried; no blood was shed.

A quiet, impeccable labor
brought forth the invisible self.

I birthed a body with my body;
then the self I thought I had

escaped. That fugitive fled
through no birth canal;

it deserted me after
the afterbirth—

pushed out not
by the baby

but the forms of labor
she occasioned:

Patting her back for an hour
so she'd nap. Puréeing peas

and sweet potatoes. Washing clothes.
Washing more clothes.

Marx on the alienation of labor
seemed a proper antidote.

I read the body-loving feminists too,
and I wanted to relate.

But I longed, really, for the souls
men got to have.

Descartes' *I think, therefore I am.*
Jesus' *I Am the Light of the World.*

The self-centeredness it took
to say the words the savior said—

the self-centeredness that gets
read as *self-*

sacrifice is what I envy,
what I want,

what no
woman I know

gets to have.

THE BOOK EATERS

My envy of the insects took me by surprise.

Whether they spotted "a spike of wheat"
or "the barren soil" in a field of words,
they found no difference:

The letter became a crumb.
The sentence became a loaf.

Blank margins metamorphosed into a soil
ever-fecund, ever-teeming with crops
as larval bodies translated
pages into food and themselves
into the winged stage.

As the baby drinks my milk,
I read. I wait to harvest
from ideas my sustenance.

I wait for my new selves to come.

OPERETTA

Scarlet blossoms coax the hummingbird's
long-beaked hunger. Beside the bloom:
a flurry. Motion obscures

the wings that make the motion.

The deep-throated flower mocks
the tenor on stage. No sound needed to lure
a beauty, the winged one, in.

I hold my child's hunger in my skin.

Am I the flower or the bird

as, from another room, I feel her cry
red-faced and hot
before she opens into sound?

A string in my chest tightens.

My feet sprout wings to meet her.

AN OPEN SPACE: *O SPAÇO ABERTO*

The baby begins to babble:
ba ba ba ba
I begin to wonder—
does the mouth close and open,
by chance or through a gesture,
yet I feel pressure:
My Portuguese is fading.
Fala com ela em português!
Por favor!
Look at that little duck—
patinho amarelinho
and she smiles and says, *pa pa*
circling around an open space
that looks for a name

Syllables utter themselves:
ma ma ma ma
do I hear a term of endearment—
closing, now, precisely around my role,
deliberate, like an embrace,
I need my mother tongue to fill my mouth.
My mother pleads,
Speak to your daughter in Portuguese!
So I say to my daughter: *Olha para o patinho—*
patinho pequeno (words I'll place beside the yellow duck
in the closet as soon as the bath is done)
pa pa, she says as the water drains. I think of language
that encompasses families, migrations, and a toy duck
to crack open our stories

SELF-PORTRAIT AS A WOMAN'S INTENTION TO WRITE

once she gives birth once the feeding's over
once the baby sleeps once the crying
stops once the clothes are clean once the piles
are folded once her old clothes fit once the mind
is clear once the baby babbles once intention
buds once fatigue fades once the new
day starts once her body's hers once the toddler
speaks once an hour cracks open
once the words surround her once a poem
grips her once the child's at school
once the woman's cry is louder than the child's

THE PITTED BONES

I thread this voice through the tiny holes in the pelvic bones
of the women who have labored.

I'm not sure what you will hear from the other side.

Leaning into a strange-sounding whistle,
you may notice:

it doesn't rise to the force of the wind.

I think often of you men
who howl and yawp and gather all the leaves in the wind
of your voices.

All of you and all of me, we
threaded our giant bodies through a woman's
at some point.

Or, we were cut out
of boneless wombs that bled.

(We tried to make space for ourselves.)

I want for art to mirror life, but there's a problem,
you see, with mirrors:
their flatness reflects us flatly.

So I sing my little tune through a skeleton's grooves,

and art enters the world as life does,
through a hollow too small for the skull—

just right for the width of this voice.

III

A FAMILY OF TREES

THE MARROW

I want to know how I'll be known.

So I read. I read of archaeologists
spotting pockmarks along the inside
of a skeleton's pelvic inlet.

Craters point to trauma, torn ligaments.

In other words, a child was born.

From those tiny dents, the experts extract
a story of birth as if it were the marrow
of a woman's life, alive in her dead body's bones.

Those holes will tell my story too.

But here's what they won't say:

I'd imagined my tale as one that covered its holes
like fingers on a flute, releasing long,
lyrical phrases that extend our breaths
past their usual ins and outs,
reaching toward a desire that knows
no punctuation or logic or knowledge of death.

Unlike ligaments, this narrative would not tear.

I must admit my work has yet to reach completion.

Someone—a parent, a child—
cries out always
in the middle of my labor.

MOTHER OF METAPHOR

As a mother, she refers to herself in the third person.
Mama's here. Don't cry. Mama's coming.
Her voice becomes a room for others.
Mama's going outside, she says, when the room is filled
to capacity. She heads to the porch looking out
at the maple tree no one ever made a fuss about.
Two squirrels chase each other in spirals around the trunk.
They chitter like bickering siblings. A hole in the tree
resolves the argument like a tired mother when one squirrel
climbs in and the other's crowded out. He goes looking
for his purpose. He leaps toward a robin on the lawn.
He skips like a stone across water, across the grass,
lifting a winged maple seed into tufts of fur.
The body becomes a vehicle for another's ambitions.
Mama's going back inside now, tired of being a hole in a tree,
a squirrel in a hole, a traveler in search of an aim—
a vehicle for metaphors the poet will affix
to her body, which she will carry for a while.

SMALL GREEN BOWL

At eighteen months, my daughter says,
Do you want more? when she wants
more grapes, more blueberries,
more cubes of cheese
to fill her small green plastic bowl.

Do you want to get up?
Do you want to go out?
Do you want to listen to that song again?

These are the questions I ask her,
which she repeats. No *I*
comes to fill the small green plastic bowl.

Mama speaks of herself as *Mama*—
and Mama's child is always *you.*

As you learn to search yourself for the small
green plastic bowl, I find
an *I*, as do you.

We fill the bowl together with cold berries.

AGREEABLE SUBJECTS

When a past father of mine makes an appearance
in my current father's sentences,
I welcome him and pay attention to the language
comprising his person.

My scrutiny will help me to know
when the past father departs in the near future
as he is wont to do.

The subjects and verbs of this father's clauses agree.

They are agreeable subjects,
obeying his commands.

I pose questions to them:
Where were you yesterday
in the morning, when my father woke up, disoriented,
and you became *this* or *that*
inside a vague pronoun,
detached from its antecedent?

Subjects:
It is important that you tether yourselves
to real things in the world—
the snowman my daughter called a "snow*person*,"
who has prunes for eyes and a berry mouth.
The flicker that perches daily
on a sunlit spot on our leafless maple.

It is important, too, that I not get my hopes up.

Language connects the past father to me.
That father, *this* father—
language delivers them both.

Sometimes I can't
distinguish between them.

PORTRAIT OF APHASIA AS A ROW OF SHELLS

Was it not then, as you ebbed from conversation
like an ocean at low tide, I found myself on the wet sand,
skirting dead jellyfish tangled in kelp and sticks
and haloed by small insects. I walked a long time.
Which is to say I could not join you in the pool
of language where we'd immersed ourselves before.
Peeling shards of shells from the sodden beach,
I scavenged my mind for metaphors to give me refuge
from your silences. So many memories had forsaken you.
The intact husks of creatures called me in their ghostly way:
they'd contained whole lives they did not remember.
I needed to keep them, hear them clicking in my pockets.
I needed to line them up on the shore of a poem:
here and here and here and here—

SELF-PORTRAIT AS A CLOTHESLINE

My life was stretched between two sweet gum trees.

Moments hung from me, the ones memory kept,
pinched between clothespins, flapping:

A clean wet sock
(a first love)
black with a yellow stripe across the toes.

A blouse the wind sent wrapping around the line
(a loss that hid from me
my life for some time).

Some pins held up
nothing (a dream of
a future, whole days
I missed) as a gust
lifts a sheet onto someone's lawn.

Once, sharp talons gripped the line—
a sparrow, perching.
Its head twitched left and right
as though it didn't intend its life.

Then the sparrow, lifting off,
plucked the cord,
made it ripple, made clothes swing.

And there I was
again,
between the trees.

FROM YOUR CHEST TO MINE

After the weaning, after my milk became a recollection
of an ache, of a tingling plenitude visiting me in waves,
of milk ducts clogged and myself plugged shut
with another's hunger—was it not then,
once I believed myself receptive again—
my senses the inlets I'd always known them to be—
my mother phoned me, her voice weighty,
urgent, though she laughed and dithered
as if lighter words could bend to circumvent
an inner impasse. Then, leaden words escaped—
gave shape to a lump in her breast.
Cancer of the milk duct.
I took that tumor in like a sickening
milk I could not stomach—myself an adult
glutted with this knowledge, my arms
pin-pricked and aching, my chest freighted
with a future I could not, in this body, hold.

PORTRAIT OF MY PARENTS IN INVISIBLE INK

I rummage through my parents' drawers
in search of a pen that works.
Curlicues test each nib in the margins.
The page's middle
I keep blank, save space for thought.
Colorless corkscrews, invisible tornadoes
frame the page like warnings in braille.
I grab more pens, etch helixes everywhere—
DNA ghosts, genetic material
for questions that go unasked.
What will I pass on?
What will I say?
I keep spiraling—I need to write
about my home, my ailing parents.
But here, so many tendrils lack a vine.

THE ROMAN ROOM METHOD

I tell my father about the mnemonic techniques
of Greek and Roman orators—

They'd construct palaces in their minds,
affixing—to this archway, to that dome—
portions of speeches they'd hope
to remember.

He needs a trick to remind him
my mom has started chemotherapy.

This is why she looks pale right now.
This is why her hair is falling out.

I need a room I can tell him to visualize—
a wall with a brass hook
where he can hang this fact
like a coat.

Or is it better to let our conversation
fall out of his head,
tangling with the whorls
of my mother's hair on the floor?

DEATHWATCH BEETLE, *XESTOBIUM RUFOVILLOSUM*

The deathwatch beetle makes a ticking sound
(a second hand making the rounds)

as its mandibles tap the walls of the tunnels
it has bored through the wood and books

of old houses. The beetle gets its name
from this metronomic pulse—

too quiet to be heard in the din
of daylight—audible to vigil-holders

at the bedsides of the ill.
I have not heard the clicking jaws;

the beetles have not hollowed out
my house. I have only read of them

during the hushed hours,
threading their bodies through books,

haunting the humans with their mouth sounds.
And I have felt some envy, some desire.

That my hunger pull me forward, too.
That my voice be the beetle's body,

piercing through the human fictions,
unafraid to conjure death as it moves.

SO THE PACHYDERMS THREW A PARTY

When I call the tumor in my mom's breast
a *death nugget*, do I want to make friends
with death, or am I trying to kick it
off its pedestal, humble death a bit?
And do I simply love my games of words,
or is it a weak defense against fate
that my father's shrinking hippocampus
makes me picture a college for hippos
shuttering? The future arrives quickly.
Pachyderms can't keep up with its demands.
In any case, the hippos celebrate.
Chemo is frying my mom's death nugget!
And the hippos are dancing, as they have
no school. No school for the rest of their lives!

SEQUEL

Picture books are for babies, my daughter declares,
pulling from her shelf the green caterpillar,
the blue-jacketed bear. I try to follow along,
honor this phase. In stacks, in boxes, the books
lie for days. A golden lion, king of one stack,
smiles under a bubble that says ROAR.
What's a "roar" without that sunny head?
I live in rows of black words, white pages.
Once, my daughter squealed at the black-
and-white misbehaving spotted dog
who tramples rows of flowers and is loved.
In stacks, in boxes, the books lie for days.
Here, a marigold's face can grow a mane, a lion
can bloom. A childhood can end, begin again.

ORDER OF OPERATIONS

You try to follow your father's dictum:
Stay ahead; cover next week's chapter in algebra
now, so when the teacher delivers the lesson
in the future, the future will be a memory
for you—the word problem you've already
solved. "A family travels in a train at a velocity
x miles per hour greater than a car." From inside
the train, the car seems to slip slowly backward
like salmon swimming against the current
to spawn. But you are not chasing time
to make life. As you speed through the weeks
to the destination, you try to quantify the benefit
of an earlier arrival. You need to know why,
in the textbook of your life, the order of operations
insists that you cry for your father before he dies,
so when he dies, you are prepared. You'll live
in the memory of pain, which is not pain.
It's a family moving forward on a train.

BLUEPRINTS

I help my father build a memory palace
where I hope to be an integral part ·
of its design—the pillar that keeps the structure
from collapse. We talk of places he can still
call up in his mind. The house in Hyderabad
where he was born. A train station in Agra
where he left his youth behind.
I follow him into a Bombay movie theater:
whirring fans chill the cinema's air.
A black-and-white film pulls him in,
offers succor from the orange
heat of June. Outside, a salesman sells
overripe mangoes from a bicycle cart.
Shoeless children ask tourists for money.
A monkey clambers across a powerline.
I have never been to India, my father's
motherland. It is tricky to make myself
a vital figure there, a place I've never been,
a time before I exist. I insist
I can be airbrushed in.
Make me a child beside the monkey
tightrope-walking on the powerline—
that monkey you still remember.

ARCHIPELAGO

A clothesline suspended between two trees
seemed an apt metaphor for identity
back when the clothes nicked by a gale

stood for odd, forgotten moments,
memorable only when they blew away.
That was a few missing socks ago—

before the line let slip
moments when the body was porous,
when I was warm skin and milk for another,

when the wind snatched from my father's mind
who he is and who we used to be.
That was before a virus turned us

into warm and gracious hosts.
The line curled around our sweet gum tree,
making the tree seem central to our lives,

when it was not. I need a new
clothesline or sturdier imaginary
clothespins or a new metaphor—

one that holds our whole sieve-like bodies
and the fictions we keep trying to contain.
I need an image for what we are

when the body abandons the ego.
An archipelago? See that lovely chain
of islands resembling the points

on a connect-the-dots activity for a child.
The eye can join the islands or see
scattered masses of land that a tiny hand

has not been drawn to—
has not picked up a crayon
to make a through-line through them.

Just let the little islands be.

FIRST HAIRCUT

My calendar reminds me I'm due for a haircut.
It chimes, tells me to leave the house.
My dad's been dead two days.
I can call the place, say I can't be there—
can't have scissors snipping dead ends off
dead hair shafts. Why is this a thing the living
even do? Two negatives make a positive,
I tell myself. So I go. I'm ushered to a chair
that reclines so my neck rests on the cold rim
of a basin. A faucet turns. Water rushes.
I stare at Art Deco patterns on a tin ceiling
older than my dad will ever be.
Thin hands cradle my head as I am laved
by warm water. Oh, to have my head's weight
held like this. To be an infant again,
bathed by loving hands.

ALIGHTING

From a distance
I spot roadkill in my lane.

As I approach,
it moves:

a gray wing rises,
lowers—a sparrow

trying to fly.
I swerve and look

back, see the wind
flap a wing—

the bird, still dead. Its feathers
combed by air.

In a poem,
when a dead thing

moves, I
switch lanes too.

My father lands on a thought
like a blackbird

on a powerline. Its talons
sharp. I am

busy. I am writing a poem
about a bird on a road. I

drop down to the next line—

MEMORY WING

My friend who is admitted to the institution's memory wing
talks to me on the phone and makes my father hover
on the wing of a memory like dust from a shaken blanket
as the friend rambles like he did,
losing me mostly, tugging me back with a sudden joke
as he says, *How quaint, this new address of mine:*
Room 125 of the Memory Wing, and I laugh.
I ask of the building's capacity—how many rooms it holds—
and he can't remember and laughs at his lapse.
He claims the rooms are many, housing people whose coughs
escape past closed doors to invade his dreams at night.
I don't belong here, my friend declares.
He is a philosopher, so I ask him a hefty question,
expecting it'll buoy him awhile: *What does it mean, to* belong?
I wait for him to descant interminably as he usually does,
the way my father always did when he found
doors opening to halls down which old thoughts had trodden.
He closes the door, stays silent, as if to answer:
What makes a person belong is a complex matter,
but what is simple is this: belonging is not
for the memory wing. This is where you go when time wings past
and stops going inside you—stops entering the rooms altogether.

A BIRD IN THE MIND

The trees, the redwoods, waving, skimmed her thought of the trees
the way the wind grazed the canopy of the forest.
Some trunks creaked as her mind fell quiet,
heightening to the falling capacity of trees
that stand at such a height. Her mind-tree leaned till it fell,
and her mind-ear leaned till it heard
the sound the tree might make if it tipped,
if it brushed the other trees' leaves
and then branches and then whatever ground would catch it
when it toppled, cutting a hole in the mind-forest's top.
Light flooded the space. She was happy.
Death had hollowed her out, making spaces within her
as the redwoods have, which animals entered and filled with themselves.
Some were clawed, and by digging, made the hollows wider.
Some had wings that flapped and tickled her as they flew
up until they'd gotten a bird's-eye view of the uppermost layer
of that forest. They were higher than the woman was
and higher than the tree had been. Free enough to flee her.
And free enough within to stay within.

THE TREES THAT POINTED TO TREES

The author reviews the pages she's written.
When she comes upon a scene where the heroine
mourns the self she'd thought was stable,
she resolves to pluck the character from the tale.
Remarkably, nothing is lost when the figure
who equated change with loss departs. Shifts
in light—encroaching shadows—stop foreshadowing
human sadness. The landscapes grow lusher
with the deletion of the static self—the diction,
more crystalline as the pen traces redwood trunks
narrowing at their tops like needles. Words
thread themselves through a circle of trees
called a *cathedral* or a *family*, formed when a single tree
falls and its branches reach upward to the light,
seeming to become freestanding trees of their own.
Now that the drama is gone from her story,
the trees will stand for trees alone.

THE CIGARETTE BEETLE'S BILDUNGSROMAN

It comes to pass that pinholes through the book's cover
signify a departure—
of beetles.

It comes to pass that, using hunger to carve secret passageways,
the beetle bores its way through the larval stage,
arriving, pupated, at the book's end.

Trails of paper powder spill in the beetle's wake.
Words scatter like ash
flicked from a cigarette.

It comes to pass that a beetle
passes through a love story mostly unscathed:
a protagonist of a bildungsroman,
molting old abrasions.

Hungers tempered, the beetle shucks
the exoskeleton the book had become,
prepared to greet the real world,
complete.

NOTES

➤ "Wash That Man Right Out of My Hair": The title is adapted from the song "I'm Gonna Wash That Man Right Outa My Hair," written by Oscar Hammerstein II and Richard Rodgers for the 1949 musical *South Pacific*.

➤ "Wash That Man Right Out of My Hair": The epigraph is taken from Ingri and Edgar Parin D'Aulaire, *D'Aulaires' Book of Greek Myths* (New York: Bantam Doubleday Dell Publishing Group Inc., 1962), p. 34.

➤ "Phantom": The epigraph is taken from Silas Weir Mitchell, *Injuries of Nerves and Their Consequences* (Philadelphia: J.B. Lippincott & Co., 1872), p. 348.

➤ "Phantom": The quote attributed to René Descartes is taken from his letter to Libert Froidmont, Belgian theologian and scientist, October 3, 1637, in René Descartes, *The Philosophical Writing of Descartes, Volume III: The Correspondence*, trans. John Cottingham et al. (Cambridge: Cambridge University Press, 1991), p. 64.

➤ "Real Estate": The aphorism "Every man is born as many men and dies as a single one" is widely attributed to Martin Heidegger, though the quote is not sourced to Heidegger's writings.

➤ "Jesus Envy": The well-known quote widely attributed to Jesus refers to the New Revised Standard Version Bible, John 8:12 and John 9:5.

➤ "Jesus Envy": The quote attributed to René Descartes is taken from Part IV of his *Discourse on Method* (1637).

ACKNOWLEDGMENTS

Thank you to the editors of the following journals, where earlier or current iterations of these poems appeared:

AGNI: "A Vase on a Shelf"
Alaska Quarterly Review: "Portrait of Aphasia on a Plum Tree"
Beloit Poetry Journal: "The Book Eaters"
Blackbird: "Archipelago" and "Sonetto"
The Carolina Quarterly: "A Bird in the Mind"
The Cincinnati Review: "Language, a Meal I Thought We Shared," "Nesting," "The Pitted Bones," and "The Roman Room Method"
Diode: "Blueprints" and "A Cord to Bind Us"
Feminist Studies: "Achilles Sees Life Leaving from His Heel" and "Wash That Man Right Out of My Hair"
Four Way Review: "Self-Portrait as the Cornfields"
The Journal: "Operetta"
The Missouri Review "Poem of the Week": "Possible Consolation of a Brain Scan's Topography"
New Ohio Review: "The Culprit," "Partition," and "The Stories That Told You"
Plume Poetry Journal: "Agreeable Subjects"
Poetry Northwest: "Eternal Pistachios"
Prairie Schooner: "Phantom"
West Branch: "The Marrow"

Thank you a million times, Rebecca Olander and Perugia Press, for selecting *The Book Eaters* as the 2023 Perugia Press Prize winner. Rebecca: How fortunate I am to work with such an attentive, scrupulous editor. You have taken such care to support my manuscript's metamorphosis into a book. May it sprout wings and find its readers!

So much gratitude to Catherine Barnett, Victoria Chang, and Paisley Rekdal for ushering *The Book Eaters* into the world with your words.

Thank you, Elizabeth Munger, for creating an image for this cover that captures the spirit of my poems.

Thank you, Jeff Potter, for bestowing upon *The Book Eaters* your time and your graphic design expertise and artistry. What a beautiful book you've helped create!

Many thanks to the following institutions whose scholarships made possible my participation in vibrant writing communities: Bread Loaf Writers' Conference, Community of Writers, Napa Valley Writers' Conference, the Rona Jaffe Foundation, and Tin House Summer Writers' Workshop. I am also indebted to my colleagues in the Goodrich Scholarship Program at UNO: thank you for supporting my participation in conferences and for giving me hope in our community as we serve the program's mission.

Thank you to all of my poetry teachers. Victoria Chang: when I read your work, I feel closer to myself and moved to write. Through reading your poetry, I've discovered new possibilities for the elegiac mode. Brenda Hillman, Kathleen Peirce, and Paisley Rekdal: thank you for imparting to me your deep knowledge and attention to craft.

Shout-out to my poetry compatriots! Our ongoing conversations keep me company as I venture onto the blank page. Rhoni Blankenhorn, Laura Cresté, Asa Drake, Shelby Handler, Kari Hawkey, Sara Mae, L.A. Johnson, Nicole W. Lee, Carling McManus, Laura Passin, Jimin Seo, Donna Spruijt-Metz, Joannie Stangeland, Weiji Wang, Alice White, and Alison Zheng: thank you for enriching my life as you do.

I am particularly grateful to my friends who read the entirety of *The Book Eaters* in earlier forms and offered feedback. Asa Drake, Mary Marbourg, Jivin Misra, Joannie Stangeland, Todd Richardson, and Alice White: *The Book Eaters* was nourished by your time and keen insights.

Alice White: you are the poetry friend I'd always sought and never thought I'd find. Thank you for reading and rereading every phrase I've asked you to consider; thank you for mirroring my obsessions to such an extent that, with you, I feel normal! How grateful I am to have found a kindred spirit in you.

Thank you to my family and friends, near and far—to the extended Hotchandani family, the Araujos, the Mungers: I am lucky that I have had the steady support of so many while writing this book, and always. To Arienne, my little one: you brighten my world; your gleeful curiosity and delight in life sustain me. To Mark, my beloved, my partner in life—thank you for innumerable gestures of love and for the feeling that inspires them. Thank you for opening your eyes to my bright computer screen all the times I've interrupted your sleep for the sake of my poems. If that's not love, I don't know what is.

Finally, thank you to my dear parents, whose strength, passion, and tenderness constitute all that I am and give to the world.

ABOUT THE AUTHOR

Carolina Hotchandani is a Latinx/South Asian poet born in Brazil and raised in various parts of the United States. She holds degrees from Brown, Texas State, and Northwestern universities and has received scholarships from the Bread Loaf Writers' Conference, Community of Writers, Napa Valley Writers' Conference, the Rona Jaffe Foundation, and Tin House Writers' Workshop. Her poetry has appeared in *AGNI*, *Alaska Quarterly Review*, *Beloit Poetry Journal*, *Blackbird*, *Cincinnati Review*, *Missouri Review*, *Prairie Schooner*, and other journals. She is a Goodrich Assistant Professor of English in Omaha, Nebraska, where she lives with her husband and daughter.

ABOUT PERUGIA PRESS

Perugia Press publishes one collection of poetry each year, by a woman at the beginning of her publishing career. Our mission is to produce beautiful books that interest longtime readers of poetry and welcome those new to poetry. We also aim to celebrate and promote poetry whenever we can, and to keep the cultural discussion of poetry inclusive.

Also from Perugia Press:

- *American Sycamore*, Lisbeth White
- *Through a Red Place*, Rebecca Pelky
- *Now in Color*, Jacqueline Balderrama
- *Hail and Farewell*, Abby E. Murray
- *Girldom*, Megan Peak
- *Starshine Road*, L. I. Henley
- *Brilliance, Spilling: Twenty Years of Perugia Press Poetry*
- *Guide to the Exhibit*, Lisa Allen Ortiz
- *Grayling*, Jenifer Browne Lawrence
- *Sweet Husk*, Corrie Williamson
- *Begin Empty-Handed*, Gail Martin
- *The Wishing Tomb*, Amanda Auchter
- *Gloss*, Ida Stewart
- *Each Crumbling House*, Melody S. Gee
- *How to Live on Bread and Music*, Jennifer K. Sweeney
- *Two Minutes of Light*, Nancy K. Pearson
- *Beg No Pardon*, Lynne Thompson
- *Lamb*, Frannie Lindsay
- *The Disappearing Letters*, Carol Edelstein
- *Kettle Bottom*, Diane Gilliam
- *Seamless*, Linda Tomol Pennisi
- *Red*, Melanie Braverman
- *A Wound On Stone*, Faye George
- *The Work of Hands*, Catherine Anderson
- *Reach*, Janet E. Aalfs
- *Impulse to Fly*, Almitra David
- *Finding the Bear*, Gail Thomas

The text of this book is set in Cormorant Garamond, an open-source type family published by Google Fonts and designed and produced in Zürich by Christian Thalmann and Catharsis Fonts. This delicate oldstyle serif family is loosely inspired by classical Garamond letterforms and brings an idiosyncratic and beautiful energy to the printed page. The book title and poem headings are set in Reforma 1969, one of three related type families developed by Alejandro Lo Celso and Pampa Type in Argentina and commissioned by the Universidad Nacional de Córdoba. The type families—ranging from a classical but contemporary serif family (Reforma 1918) to a humanist sans serif family (Reforma 2018), with Reforma 1969 as a semi-sans in between—were developed as open-source software in the spirit of the Argentinian national policy of open, free, and inclusive education.